God, Who Are You?

~~~~~~~~~~~~

Jeannette Altes
~~~~~~~~~~~~

God, Who Are You? / Jeannette Altes – 1st Ed.
ISBN-13: 978-1983824814

Contents

Dedicated to my closest friend ~

Immanuel ~ God With Us

The Character of God

"Who said anything about safe?
'Course he isn't safe.
But he's good. He's the King, I tell you."
C. S. Lewis,
The Lion, the Witch and the Wardrobe

When I began working on this project, the first question was: where do I start? After a little thought, it seemed the place to begin should be God, Himself. Who is He? What is He like? What is the character of God? Big questions? Yes, but also foundational questions. Really, the answer to these questions form the foundations of our beliefs and view of how the world works. So, let us begin….

The first thing, I think, that should be clarified, is how we view God. Or, what kind of God are we looking for? If you are confused, I understand. Let me explain. The real God, the God revealed, progressively, through the Scriptures, is often not the God we are taught about in church. In my experience, the God we are taught in church, in Sunday School, that is projected out by the church, is a neatly packaged easily defined god that fits in the world view box of his creators. In short, he is safe. And this is not surprising. We humans value greatly predictability and knowing what to expect – having things lined up and in order. It gives the illusion of safety. But honestly, I have come to realize that a god I can fully define and fully understand isn't really a god at all. If I can understand him, then he is not greater than any man, or really, less so as I can't pretend that I truly understand anyone fully, myself included. So if I cannot even understand myself, why would it make sense that I could fully define and package who God is? To me, it doesn't. And this was a difficult thing to learn.

One of the starting places for me coming to this understanding actually began with events that proved to me – repeatedly – that the church and the leaders of the church were not what they taught me to believe they were. They were not trustworthy, infallible, above the pew-sitters, no. And this presented a problem because I had been raised to believe that the Institutional Church (IC) and God were synonymous – that if I walked away from the IC, I was walking away from God. And yet not once, but three times, I had no choice if I wanted to maintain my sanity and any sense of integrity. This sense that God and the IC are irrevocably intertwined has been a part of the IC culture for a very long time – multiplied centuries. And people have become so invested in the god of their particular box that wars have been fought and people have been executed. For what? Well, really, these wars and such are for the accumulation and consolidation of power, aren't they? Temporal power. Control over people and resources… money. And you will pursue and serve whichever master you choose. And this brings me back to the need to understand who God really is – what He is like.

The following passage from Isaiah in The Message hit me between the eyes a few years ago. It has slowly, but surely altered my perspective and helped me let go of my learned bullet points about God:

> *"So to whom will you compare me,*
> *the Incomparable?*
> *Can you picture me without reducing me?"*
> *Isaiah 46:5 The Message*

And this is what I began to understand: there is no one and nothing that can be used as a method of comparison to fully understand God because there is no one that even comes close to being like Him…and that every effort we make to try and picture Him is going to be incomplete – reducing Him – because we are not capable of fully comprehending who and what God is. This may sound simple – like a "well, duh!" kind of thing. But it really is not. I think all of us, if we take a moment and examine what we believe about God and who He is, will find that we have made the assumption that what we have been taught is the whole – the sum – and there is no more. A nice, neat box with a pretty little bow that must not be questioned – safe…

But God will not fit in our nice little boxes. I think, when we open them and examine them closely – honestly – we will find them mostly empty, or at best, incomplete and lacking depth. In fact, what I realized when I began to look in my boxes – both the ones I had been given and the ones I created myself – was that mostly what was in there was something that was created in the image of man – something that was nice and safe. Naturally. The only frame of reference we have for God is seen through the filter of ourselves. And we are, after all, created in His image. He said so Himself. So, then, He must be like us....wait...no... When pondered, this is actually a terrifying thought. Because if God is like us, then He would be inconsistent, fallible, capricious, play favorites, seek revenge (as opposed to justice), overlook those in need, reward with material wealth and/or fame, be distracted, make mistakes... In fact, he would not be God at all. Where does that leave us?

Well, to back up a bit, I think it is normal – expected, even – that we would want a God we can understand, a God that is like us. We want a God that makes sense and feels safe in human terms. But that is not the God we need. We need a God that is much bigger that we are – more just, more powerful, more understanding, wiser, stronger, deeper, higher, more alive, more stable...in short, we need the God that created us, not the god we created for ourselves. And that is a big difference.

So, who is this God that created us? I think one of the foundational issues in this comes in understanding or knowing the character of God. I have observed, over the years, no small amount of heated debate on this topic. The first challenge to man's relationship with God was one that, in its essence, called into question God's character.

> *"Then the serpent said to the woman, "You will not surely die. For God knows that in the day you eat of it your eyes will be opened, and you will be like God, knowing good and evil."*
> *So when the woman saw that the tree was good for food, that it was pleasant to the eyes, and a tree desirable to make one wise, she took of its fruit and ate. She also gave to her husband with her, and he ate."*
>
> *Genesis 3:4-6 NKJV*

In this narrative, it is implied that the reason for the command not to eat from the tree is that God is afraid that man will become like him. That is, it implies God is holding a beneficial thing back from man out of fear of being overshadowed and cast aside: that God is, in fact, deceptive and a liar. Now, on the surface, this sounds pretty ridiculous. I know. But it is said much more subtly than that. "Did God really say? Did God really mean?" The intent is not to convince outright but to just insinuate doubt. It is that subtle suggestion that rather than being for us, God is against us. That rather than being our advocate, He is our adversary. It asks if God really loves us, cares for us, trusts us. In short, it questions if His character can really be trusted.

That brings us to the place of needing to understand what God's character is. For me, with the wide variety of theologies I was hearing, and platitudes that did not comfort, and church people that did not really care, it became imperative for me to really settle the foundation of God's character. If I was going to trust Him, I mean *really* trust Him with my life, I had to know if His character was worthy of that trust. That statement got me in trouble a few times with the more religious people that I encountered. But the thing is, trust must be merited. In our human relationships, we expect trust to be earned. And we trust based on demonstrated character. So how do we know the

Character of God? The scriptures actually have quite a bit to say about that. And that is a good place to start.

There are many places throughout the scriptures that describe God. There have been many books written about it and there are even posters that list many of them. They are the names of God. These are the various progressive ways He revealed Himself to man through the ages and we gave Him names accordingly: "the God who…" or "the God of…" These names are revelations of His character. He is Just. He is Righteous. He is Good. He is Perfect. He is Peace. He is Healer. He is Provider. He is Father. He is Nurturer. He is Protector. He is Jealous. He is a Consuming Fire. He is Merciful. He is Refuge. He is Strength. He is Wisdom. He is Great. He is Majestic. He is Judge. He is King of All. He is Salvation. He is Holy. He is Pure. He is the Lord. He is Truth. He is the Way. He is Life. He is Faithful. He is One. He is Witness. He is Light. He is all these things and more. And all of these things are like the many facets on an exquisitely and perfectly cut diamond. Each facet reflecting an aspect of who He is. But the core, the foundation of it all, the fire in the center of the diamond that lights up the many facets…that is represented in the name Immanuel – God With Us. Why is this name the core representation of God's character? Because it represents Jesus. And there is no greater expression of this core of God's character than Jesus. This core is Love. God is Love. It is His Love that drives everything He does. All other aspects – facets – of His character must be viewed through this core, this Fire, this Light of Love.

> *"He who does not love does not know God, for God is love. In this the love of God was manifested toward us, that God has sent His only begotten Son into the world, that we might live through Him."*
>
> *1 John 4:8-9 NKJV*

> *"Love has been perfected among us in this: that we may have boldness in the day of judgment; because as He is, so are we in this world. There is no fear in love; but perfect love casts out fear, because fear involves torment. But he who fears has not been made perfect in love. We love Him because He first loved us."*
>
> *1 John 4:17-19 NKJV*

And when we learn of His Love – when we experience His Love personally, we learn that we can trust Him. We learn that we can trust His character with our very lives. We learn that His Love drives Him to be presently, purposefully, active in our lives. We learn that although, in human terms, He is not safe, He is fundamentally and foundationally and wholly Good. When we talk to Him, He hears us. He cares when we cry and when we laugh. He is a true Parent of whom even the best human parents are a mere shadow. His capacity for Love is greater than ours – He loves each of us deeply; more deeply and perfectly than the most devoted human parent is capable of when they love their child. He loves us more than our ability to believe or imagine – that is, His love for us and His ability and desire to act on our behalf are not limited by our capacity to believe in it or imagine it. And He proved that love – the depths of that character – by leaving Heaven, taking on the flesh of a man – going through the process of being born and growing up – taking the time to teach of Himself, demonstrate His love through miracles. And the ultimate expression of love – He laid down His life and died for us, His children, His friends. The cross and the resurrection – Immanuel – God With Us. Choosing to forever become human – forever binding Himself to us –

and in so doing, forever elevating us to Him. Love. Love that never falters or wavers. That is God's character. And when we begin to get that – to understand it, we can begin to relax and trust Him.

> *"And now abide faith, hope, love, these three; but the greatest of these is love."*
> *1 Corinthians 13:13 NKJV*

Who Do You Follow?

"He who begins by loving Christianity, better than truth, will proceed by loving his own sect or church better than Christianity, and end in loving himself better than all."
Samuel Taylor Coleridge

What is the foundational concept of Christianity? What is the essential purpose? Ask this question of a hundred people and you will probably get a hundred different answers. Over the years, my own definition has changed. Some say, "You must believe a, b, and c; go to one of our approved churches that is connected to our established organization." Others will respond, "No, no, no! You *must* believe x, y, and z and *never* associate with people who go to *that* church." Sigh.

There are so many different points of view on what being a Christian is. It seems, in my experience, that many who claim the title "Christian," especially in the West, when asked what their religion is, respond with the name of their denomination or particular organization: Baptist,

Assemblies of God, Pentecostal, Catholic, Lutheran, Anglican, and on and on. And really, I guess this is accurate. The rules and rites and traditions of our particular denomination are, by definition, religious exercises. And this defines what it means to be a Baptist or a Pentecostal or a Catholic. But it seems to kind of confuse what it means to be a Christian.

This led to a different question: who do you follow? Interestingly, this also can get you a lot of different answers: Calvin, Luther, the Pope, Hagin, Sproul, Piper, MacPherson, Pierce – the list could go on and on. Again, it seems people who claim the name "Christian" are identifying most with a specific doctrinal teaching by a specific religious leader. And it is not a bad thing to read the experiences and teachings of people we respect concerning what they have learned. I spent time answering these questions this way for many years. But again, the question rose in me, asking me, "Who do you follow?"

I know for me, a lot of what was in my mind when I would answer with a denomination or a religious leader was the feeling of belonging, of being in the know and accepted into the chosen group – the group that I believed had the answers and would protect me, give me security…. Whew! That can get twisty and complicated because these aren't usually conscious thoughts and motivations. After time, with that question gently but persistently rising – "Who do you follow?" – I began to realize that I was focusing my vision, my heart, my loyalty too low.

The thing is, with so many different doctrines, how do we know which one is right? They can't all be right. It seems that in many cases, the denominations have become sort of pyramid schemes, with the doctrinal statements being at the top and the founders/leaders next. Some of these doctrinal statements are detailed and lengthy enough to fill a book or multiple books. With every internal disagreement that comes up, a new doctrinal statement must be written to address and settle it. And so it grows…and grows…. and grows… until most people don't even really know what all the doctrinal stands are within their chosen group. Interestingly, this is the very way the Midrash was written – the Jewish rules to follow the Law.

And of course, as these things get set in stone and codified, it becomes in the best interest of the organization to insure adherence to these statements within the organization. Rules. Laws. Hmm…..it almost seems like the denominations become more of a religious brand than anything else. And this leads to merchandising. And this is big business. And people start wearing symbols and buying logoed products, even logoed and approved bibles, to identify with their chosen brand and the meaning of the symbols is diluted….lost…. "Who do you follow?"

> *"In the beginning the church was a fellowship of men and women centering on the living Christ. Then the church moved to Greece where it became a philosophy. Then it moved to Rome where it became an institution. Next, it moved to Europe where it became a culture. And finally, it moved to America where it became an enterprise."*
>
> *Richard Halverson,*
> *former chaplain of the U. S. Senate*

This is where I began to have an internal problem. I was raised in a specific denomination – taught that it was the closest to the Truth. I became involved with a number of different churches over the years, all who said the same thing – we have the closest teaching to the Truth. And this isn't surprising really. People don't believe and follow a doctrine if they don't believe it to be the truth. But I began to see cracks in the foundation. Certain parts of the doctrines in all these different churches didn't feel true. Something was off on a fundamental level. The basics were true – all of them had the same basic doctrine: Jesus Christ and Him crucified, as Paul put it (1 Corinthians 2:2). But then they piled so much more onto this and the more was very contradictory. Who was right? Who was wrong? Again, the question arose in me, "Who do you follow?" And this passage came to mind as a place to start….

> *"And when he had found him, he brought him to Antioch. So it was that for a whole year they assembled with the church and taught a great many people. And the disciples were first called Christians in Antioch."*
>
> *Acts 11:26 NKJV*

What stood out to me was the last sentence. They did not call themselves Christians – those who observed them gave them this name. Why? What was observed that caused this name to be given? It seems obvious. It is obvious, really. The definition of Christian is "Christ follower." Oh! Well, then. The question becomes much more personal and significant now: "Who do you follow?" And for me, I had to ask myself why my automatic answer was not Christ. The answer was that most of us are taught to follow a doctrine, a denomination, a collection of rules, a man. In many cases, we have lost sight of the whole point, assuming we were ever taught it to begin with. What is that point? To turn from what we were following and follow Christ – to follow Jesus.

Now, following a religion, a set of rules, a religious guru…this is easy to understand. And it is – or becomes – comfortable. The parameters are clearly defined and the human need to just have a list of things to tick off as accomplished to make us feel safe, justified, in the right – righteous – is strong and even intoxicating. "Just tell me what to do and I'll do it and then we'll be all set" – comfortable in our belief that we have met the criteria and are secure. I came across the following in the Bible and it resonated loudly in me.

> *"I bring this up because some from Chloe's family brought a most disturbing report to my attention—that you're fighting among yourselves! I'll tell you exactly what I was told: You're all picking sides, going around saying, "I'm on Paul's side," or "I'm for Apollos," or "Peter is my man," or "I'm in the Messiah group." I ask you, "Has the Messiah been chopped up in little pieces so we can each have a relic all our own? Was Paul crucified for you? Was a single one of you baptized in Paul's name?"""*
>
> *1 Corinthians 1:11-13 The Message*

I think it is human nature to want a leader we can see and follow that will give us rules for being accepted. I spent a lot of years in that pursuit – trying to get my thoughts and behavior lined up just right so that I would be 'good enough' – looking to this or that celebrity preacher to give me the right formula. The thing is, it never really worked. No matter how religiously I tried to follow the rules, I never got them all right and I never felt fully satisfied. In fact, in each case, it usually ended in greater or lesser forms of spiritual disaster.

It makes me think of the point where Israel asks the prophet, Samuel, to appoint for them a king. They felt that they were somehow looked down on and lesser for not having a king like the surrounding nations did. Samuel warned them that it would not be all sunshine and roses with a king – that this king would be a tyrant over them, take from them, and it would not go well. But they were determined. Samuel went to God and was very upset. God told him that they were not rejecting Samuel, they were rejecting God, Himself, as their King (see 1 Samuel 8). But it seems to me we do the same today. Why? It is so much easier to follow an earthly leader we can see with our natural eyes and hear with our natural ears. It is easier to follow a set of black and white, bullet point instructions from men than to develop the spiritual eyes and ears. Many are never even taught that there is a difference.

But following Christ requires a sacrificial commitment. And having the desire to make that commitment requires a relationship. And a relationship requires time – an investment of time and a willingness to learn…to be a student. And I realized that just as Jesus said to His disciples nearly 2000 years ago, He was saying to each of us individually – to me, now, "Come, follow Me…."

> *"Are you tired? Worn out? Burned out on religion? Come to me. Get away with me and you'll recover your life. I'll show you how to take a real rest. Walk with me and work with me—watch how I do it. Learn the unforced rhythms of grace. I won't lay anything heavy or ill-fitting on you. Keep company with me and you'll learn to live freely and lightly."*
>
> *Matthew 11:28-30 The Message*

Law and Grace

Mankind was not made to serve the Law.
The Law was made to serve mankind.
When we begin to sacrifice people on the altar of the Law,
We move from mercy and grace to tyranny and abuse.

Law and Grace. These are two very big words in the Christian faith. I have come to realize that understanding what they are (and what they are not) is far more important than I had been taught. Growing up in the church, I really didn't hear much in depth teaching on either of these. But they are actually pretty fundamental. If you were to sum the Bible up in two words, these two would be a good choice. I came to the realization of the importance of these two words – these concepts – as I studied the Bible and wrestled with a succession of faith crises that forced the issue. So, what are these two things and what do they mean to us as followers of Christ?

First, the Law is the Mosaic Law – the Law God dictated to Moses on Mount Sinai as recorded in Exodus, Leviticus, Numbers, and Deuteronomy. Any time, in both the Old and New Testaments, when the Law is referred to, this is what is referenced. Second, Grace, simply put, is what the various New Testament authors call the gift of Life given by Christ through His death and resurrection. Now what is the relationship between these two things? Over the last twenty years of my life, my repeated prayer has been a request for freedom. This keeps leading me back to a study of the differences and relationship between Law and Grace. What have I discovered?

Well, what I was raised in – and I think most who were raised in church were raised in some variation of this as well – was the idea that we, as Christians, are free from the requirements of the Mosaic Law. Except when we're not. I was taught that we, as good Christians, should obey the Ten Commandments. I was also taught that we should tithe. And as I thought about this and studied the Bible, it seemed to me that if we still needed to follow some of the Law, shouldn't we follow all of it – like the dietary ones (no pork, no shellfish, etc.)? I was told that Jesus showed Peter in a vision (Acts 10:9-15) that all food was clean now. Oh. Okay… But the next question that formed in my mind was,

"How do we know which parts of the Law we are supposed to follow and which parts we don't have to?" It was confusing and caused a bit of underlying anxiety. What if I'm not doing it right?

As I began to study the New Testament, it seemed that Paul was teaching that we were not under the Law anymore. At all. None of it. Hmm… But the Ten Commandments. And the Tithe. And my mind said *tilt*. And I laid it all aside until it bubbled to the surface again and demanded answers. Again. And I studied some more. And I kept being brought back to the fact that something about following parts of the Law and not all of the Law didn't fit with what Paul wrote in his letters. Before I get into what I see regarding Paul's writings on this subject, I want to back up a bit to something that the church misses a lot, I think. If you go to any Jewish rabbi and ask, "Are Gentiles (all non-Jews) under the Law of Moses?" you will almost universally get the same response, often accompanied by a laugh, "No, of course they are not."

That brings me to the fifteenth chapter of Acts. In it, a group of Jewish believers have been following Paul around and trying to convince the Gentile believers that they must follow the Mosaic Law, including being circumcised, or they were not truly accepted into the faith. This was in direct conflict with what Paul had taught the Gentiles and was causing a good deal of confusion. So, Paul went to Jerusalem and asked the church leaders there to state their belief on the matter. It was a bit of a tense situation…they argued about it for a while, then Peter stood up and reminded them of his vision and being sent to the Gentiles, and then Paul and Barnabas recounted the miracles God performed among the Gentiles. More talk (see Acts 15). In the end, they agreed with Paul and sent a letter out to all the churches. The bottom line of it…

> *"For it seemed good to the Holy Spirit, and to us, to lay upon you no greater burden than these necessary things: that you abstain from things offered to idols, from blood, from things strangled, and from sexual immorality. If you keep yourselves from these, you will do well."*
>
> *Acts 15:28-29 NKJV*

So here is the crux of the matter, to me. To begin with, if we are not Jewish, then we have *never* been obligated to the Mosaic Law. Ever. Taking that as the starting point and the above letter the Jerusalem council sent to the Gentiles, becoming a follower of Christ does not cause us to become obligated to the Law. And I can hear the protestations. The first one I hear is that Jesus said he didn't come to do away with the Law. Okay. That still does not put Gentiles under the Law. However, in order to make things clear on both sides of that coin, let's address the issue of Law and Grace anyway and start by looking at exactly what Jesus said.

> *"Do not think that I came to destroy the Law or the Prophets. I did not come to destroy but to fulfill. For assuredly, I say to you, till heaven and earth pass away, one jot or one tittle will by no means pass from the law till all is fulfilled. Whoever therefore breaks one of the least of these commandments, and teaches men so, shall be called least in the kingdom of heaven; but whoever does and teaches them, he shall be called great in the kingdom of heaven. For I say to you, that unless your righteousness exceeds the righteousness of the scribes and Pharisees,*

> *you will by no means enter the kingdom of heaven."*
>
> *Matthew 5:17-20 NKJV*

Okay, the question that arose in me was simply, "what is the difference between 'do away with' and 'fulfill?'" Well, to 'do away with' means to cancel or destroy an agreement without the terms being completed – without it being fulfilled. In a legal proceeding, this may be done, for instance, if a contract is found to be illegal. In such cases, it is declared null and void and the expectation or requirement that it be fulfilled or completed is dropped. So, the Old Testament Law or the Old Covenant (another term for contract) is not to be nullified or done away with as there is no legal fault in it. Rather, Jesus came to fulfill the covenant God made with Himself on behalf of Abraham – and to fulfill, as a legal representative of the nation of Israel, the covenant God made with Israel through the Mosaic Law.

So, what does it mean that Jesus fulfilled the Law? The image that came to me was of a man with a growing family who enters into a contract with a wealthy man to borrow money to purchase a home for his family to live in. A contract is drawn up with very precise terms that are very straightforward. A pretty standard mortgage type agreement. As time goes on, life takes turns the man did not anticipate; medical bills for an accident that injured his wife, a miscalculation on other expenses, bad choices in investments and spending, children needing special equipment for school. The man is finding it harder and harder to meet the monthly payments and starts working harder and longer. He reaches a place where he has no more to give; his body is worn out and he can no longer work enough to cover the bills. He begins missing payments. He receives a letter from the wealthy gentleman saying that, per the terms of the agreement, he and his family will have to move out and will still be held responsible for the debt owed. The man is in a hopeless position. He is sick and broke and has nowhere to turn. Now, the wealthy gentleman sends his son with a proposition. The son will pay the debt in full, fulfilling the contract and allowing the man and his family to live in the house. The son makes a new contract with the father on behalf of the man. There is only one condition: any time there is a problem or something breaks, the man should come to the son and ask for his help in fixing it. What an offer! Now, if the man accepts this offer and the son has payed the terms of the first agreement in full, is the man still bound by those original first terms made with the wealthy gentlemen? Would he expect that he would still have to make payments? Would the wealthy gentleman still expect him to make payments? No. Of course not. That contract, having been fulfilled, is no longer in effect. It is complete and put away and they are operating under a new agreement.

Okay, that was a bit of a long explanation, but I think the point is made. If an agreement or contract or covenant of Law is fulfilled, it is no longer in effect. It is not nullified, it is not done away with, it is complete. Its purpose is done and it is filed away only to be looked at to confirm that the terms are fulfilled and no further action is required.

> *"Now this is the main point of the things we are saying: We have such a High Priest, who is seated at the right hand of the throne*

of the Majesty in the heavens, a Minister of the sanctuary and of the true tabernacle which the Lord erected, and not man.

For every high priest is appointed to offer both gifts and sacrifices. Therefore it is necessary that this One also have something to offer. For if He were on earth, He would not be a priest, since there are priests who offer the gifts according to the law; who serve the copy and shadow of the heavenly things, as Moses was divinely instructed when he was about to make the tabernacle. For He said, "See that you make all things according to the pattern shown you on the mountain." But now He has obtained a more excellent ministry, inasmuch as He is also Mediator of a better covenant, which was established on better promises.

For if that first covenant had been faultless, then no place would have been sought for a second. Because finding fault with them, He says: "Behold, the days are coming, says the LORD, when I will make a new covenant with the house of Israel and with the house of Judah— not according to the covenant that I made with their fathers in the day when I took them by the hand to lead them out of the land of Egypt; because they did not continue in My covenant, and I disregarded them, says the LORD. For this is the covenant that I will make with the house of Israel after those days, says the LORD: I will put My laws in their mind and write

> *them on their hearts; and I will be their God, and they shall be My people. None of them shall teach his neighbor, and none his brother, saying, 'Know the LORD,' for all shall know Me, from the least of them to the greatest of them. For I will be merciful to their unrighteousness, and their sins and their lawless deeds I will remember no more." In that He says, "A new covenant," He has made the first obsolete. Now what is becoming obsolete and growing old is ready to vanish away."*
>
> *Hebrews 8 NKJV*

Note especially the last two sentences: a new covenant has made the old obsolete and what is becoming obsolete is ready to vanish away. Put another way:

> *"God speaks of these new promises, of this new agreement, as taking the place of the old one; for the old one is out of date now and has been put aside forever."*
>
> *Hebrews 8:13 The Living Bible*

> *"What purpose then does the law serve? It was added because of transgressions, till the Seed should come to whom the promise was made; and it was appointed through angels by the hand of a mediator. Now a mediator*

does not mediate for one only, but God is one.

Is the law then against the promises of God? Certainly not! For if there had been a law given which could have given life, truly righteousness would have been by the law. But the Scripture has confined all under sin, that the promise by faith in Jesus Christ might be given to those who believe. But before faith came, we were kept under guard by the law, kept for the faith which would afterward be revealed. Therefore the law was our tutor to bring us to Christ, that we might be justified by faith. But after faith has come, we are no longer under a tutor."

Galatians 3:19-25 NKJV

Let that sink in.

As I began to dwell on this, my mind started coming up with all sorts of arguments – all the things I'd ever been taught concerning our need to obey the Law. And it was a bit scary, to be honest. This seems like very dangerous ground. Some of the main arguments that came up were: The Gospel is built upon the Old Testament, and; We are still obligated to follow the law except for the specific ones that are mentioned by name as being done away with in the

New Testament. Okay, I'm going to address these two as they were the biggest ones.

First, the entire Old Testament points to the Gospel and it is good to know the Old Testament and the Law as a frame of reference to know what we have been set free from. But the Old Covenant and the New Covenant are not mingled – they are not the same.

> *"But now we have been delivered from the law, having died to what we were held by, so that we should serve in the newness of the Spirit and not in the oldness of the letter."*
>
> *Romans 7:6 NKJV*

> *"There is therefore now no condemnation to those who are in Christ Jesus, who do not walk according to the flesh, but according to the Spirit. For the law of the Spirit of life in Christ Jesus has made me free from the law of sin and death."*
>
> *Romans 8:1-2 NKJV*

They are separate Laws or Covenants.

But the bigger confusion for me came with the second argument. I had a pastor actual state that we were to obey all parts of the Law except for those specifically mentioned as being done away with in the New Testament. Wait. Didn't Jesus say he did not come to do away with the Law? Hmm…then the pastor listed three specific things that were mentioned as being done away with: animal sacrifices because Jesus became the perfect sacrifice, dietary restrictions because of the dream Peter had about eating 'unclean' animals as recorded in Acts 10:9-16, and circumcision as stated by Paul in 1 Corinthians 7:18-19. Okay. This made sense. At first. Until I actually started *reading* the Mosaic Law….

> *"If a man has a stubborn and rebellious son who will not obey the voice of his father or the voice of his mother, and who, when they have chastened him, will not heed them, then his father and his mother shall take hold of him and bring him out to the elders of his city, to the gate of his city. And they shall say to the elders of his city, 'This son of ours is stubborn and rebellious; he will not obey our voice; he is a glutton and a drunkard.' Then all the men of his city shall stone him to death with stones; so you shall put away*

> *the evil from among you, and all Israel shall hear and fear."*
>
> *Deuteronomy 21:18-21 NKJV*

Yikes! When I brought this up, I was told that *obviously*, that part of the Law was no longer in effect. Oh. Okay. Well, but how do we determine which parts of the Law we are still supposed to follow and which parts are no longer important? It seemed that the rule of thumb boiled down to this: we are still under the parts of the Law that we think people should be able to keep and don't violate our cultural sensibilities. Um…that seemed off, somehow….and left me always a little uneasy. How was I supposed to be sure I was keeping all the right ones? And I kept digging. And then I found this:

> *"O foolish Galatians! Who has bewitched you that you should not obey the truth, before whose eyes Jesus Christ was clearly portrayed among you as crucified? This only I want to learn from you: Did you receive the Spirit by the works of the law, or by the hearing of faith? Are you so foolish? Having begun in the Spirit, are you now being made perfect by the flesh? Have you suffered so*

many things in vain—if indeed it was in vain?

Therefore He who supplies the Spirit to you and works miracles among you, does He do it by the works of the law, or by the hearing of faith?—just as Abraham "believed God, and it was accounted to him for righteousness." Therefore know that only those who are of faith are sons of Abraham. And the Scripture, foreseeing that God would justify the Gentiles by faith, preached the gospel to Abraham beforehand, saying, "In you all the nations shall be blessed." So then those who are of faith are blessed with believing Abraham.

For as many as are of the works of the law are under the curse; for it is written, "Cursed is everyone who does not continue in all things which are written in the book of the law, to do them." But that no one is justified by the law in the sight of God is evident, for "the just shall live by faith." Yet the law is not of faith, but "the man who does them shall live by them." Christ has redeemed us from the curse of the law, having become a curse for us (for it is written, "Cursed is everyone who hangs on a tree"), that the blessing of Abraham might come upon the Gentiles in Christ Jesus, that we might receive the promise of the Spirit through faith."

Galatians 3:1-16 NKJV

> *"Stand fast therefore in the liberty by which Christ has made us free, and do not be entangled again with a yoke of bondage. Indeed I, Paul, say to you that if you become circumcised, Christ will profit you nothing. And I testify again to every man who becomes circumcised that he is a debtor to keep the whole law. You have become estranged from Christ, you who attempt to be justified by law; you have fallen from grace. For we through the Spirit eagerly wait for the hope of righteousness by faith. For in Christ Jesus neither circumcision nor uncircumcision avails anything, but faith working through love."*
>
> *Galatians 5:1-6 NKJV*

And my mind went tilt, again. Do you see it? If you try to keep one piece of the Law, you are obligated to keep it all. And worse, you are estranged from Christ. So I am led back to Jesus saying he came to fulfill the Law. And the question arose: If there are parts of the Law we are still supposed to keep, does that mean Jesus did not fulfill that piece of the Law? If the pastor that I mentioned earlier was correct, does that mean Jesus did not fulfill the Law except for those three parts? And I realized that in trying to keep even one small piece of the Mosaic Law, I was, in effect, saying that Jesus did not do what he said he would do – or that the righteousness granted to me through Jesus' death and resurrection was not sufficient and I needed to fill in the gaps.

Wow. I was stunned at this realization. And what came with this realization was that concerning the following of the Law, it is an all or nothing proposition. There is no middle ground. If we choose to follow one part of the Law, whether it be circumcision, tithing, dietary restriction, or any of the others, then we are obligated, by the Law itself and by God to follow all of the Law. We are then stating to God that we believe that we can earn our own righteousness through fulfilling the obligations of the Law ourselves. We want to be in control of our righteousness. We want to earn it. But no one, in the whole history of the human race, was ever able to keep the whole Law. No one except Jesus. And we think we can?

So what, then? Well, the only other option is to surrender to the Grace of the Law of Life in Christ Jesus. Our only hope at being righteous before God is through the finished work of Christ – the work that fulfilled all the Law. If we think that we will somehow be more righteous if we keep parts of the Law, we are miserable indeed, because no matter how hard we try, we will always mess it up somewhere, somehow. We will always fall short and feel inadequate, fearful that we are not doing it right. Or worse, we will become self-righteous and arrogant, believing we have earned our way. This is a very dangerous place to be.

> *"My old identity has been co-crucified with Messiah and no longer lives; for the nails of his cross crucified me with him. And now the essence of this new life is no longer mine, for the Anointed One lives his life through me—we live in union as one! My new life is empowered by the faith of the Son of God who loves me so much that he gave himself for me, and dispenses his life into mine! So that is why I don't view God's grace as something minor or peripheral. For if keeping the law could release God's righteousness to us, the Anointed One would have died for nothing."*
>
> *Galatians 2:20-21 TPT*

But then the question arises: surely there is some guideline, some rule that we are given. And the answer is, yes – yes there is.

> *"But when the Pharisees heard that He had silenced the Sadducees, they gathered together. Then one of them, a lawyer, asked Him a question, testing Him, and saying, "Teacher, which is the great commandment in the law?"*
> *Jesus said to him, "'You shall love the LORD your God with all your heart, with all your soul, and with all your mind.' This is the first and great commandment. And the second is like it: 'You shall love your neighbor as yourself.' On these two commandments hang all the Law and the Prophets.""*
>
> *Matthew 22:34-40 NKJV*

Hmm…so…love God and love those around you. This sums up the Law….

> *"Little children, I shall be with you a little while longer. You will seek Me; and as I said to the Jews, 'Where I am going, you cannot come,' so now I say to you.*
> *A new commandment I give to you, that you love one another; as I have loved you, that*

you also love one another. By this all will know that you are My disciples, if you have love for one another.""

John 13:33-35 NKJV

Love. As mentioned in chapter one, it is the foundation of God's character. And He wants it to be the foundation of our character, as well. As children of God through faith in Christ, we are not slaves to the Law. Christ completed the Law. It is finished. We are under a new covenant with a new law – the Law of Life in Christ, the Law of Love. Old things have passed away and Christ has made all things new.

> *"Then Jesus said to those Jews who believed Him, "If you abide in My word, you are My disciples indeed. And you shall know the truth, and the truth shall make you free."*
> *They answered Him, "We are Abraham's descendants, and have never been in bondage to anyone. How can You say, 'You will be made free'?"*
> *Jesus answered them, "Most assuredly, I say to you, whoever commits sin is a slave of sin. And a slave does not abide in the house forever, but a son abides forever. Therefore if the Son makes you free, you shall be free indeed."*
>
> *John 8:31-36 NKJV*

> *"Therefore, if you died with Christ from the basic principles of the world, why, as though living in the world, do you subject yourselves to regulations— "Do not touch, do not taste, do not handle," which all concern things which perish with the using—according to the commandments and doctrines of men? These things indeed have an appearance of wisdom in self-imposed religion, false humility, and neglect of the body, but are of no value against the indulgence of the flesh."*
>
> *Colossians 2:20-23 NKJV*

As a final thought, regardless of whether we are Jewish or not by birth or heritage, if we are following Christ, we are no longer subject to the Law. We are all equally free.

> *"For you are all sons of God through faith in Christ Jesus. For as many of you as were baptized into Christ have put on Christ. There is neither Jew nor Greek, there is neither slave nor free, there is neither male nor female; for you are all one in Christ Jesus. And if you are Christ's, then you are Abraham's seed, and heirs according to the promise."*
>
> *Galatians 3:26-29 NKJV*

The choice is before us. We either choose to rely on the Law and our ability to keep it or we rely on the Grace of God given through Jesus Christ.

> *"Not that we are sufficient of ourselves to think of anything as being from ourselves, but our sufficiency is from God, who also made us sufficient as ministers of the new covenant, not of the letter but of the Spirit; for the letter kills, but the Spirit gives life. But if the ministry of death, written and engraved on stones, was glorious, so that the children of Israel could not look steadily at the face of Moses because of the glory of his countenance, which glory was passing away, how will the ministry of the Spirit not be more glorious? For if the ministry of condemnation had glory, the ministry of righteousness exceeds much more in glory. For even what was made glorious had no glory in this respect, because of the glory that excels. For if what is passing away was glorious, what remains is much more glorious."*
>
> *2 Corinthians 3:5-11 NKJV*

The choice, then, is between the Law, which ministers death to those who try to earn their righteousness through it, and Grace, which through Christ, brings life to all who believe. And God has said from the beginning and continues to say to each of us, “Choose Life!”

> *“Most assuredly, I say to you, he who hears My word and believes in Him who sent Me has everlasting life, and shall not come into judgment, but has passed from death into life.”*
>
> *Matthew 5:24 NKJV*

God, What do you want?

> *"To have faith is to trust yourself to the water. When you swim you don't grab hold of the water, because if you do you will sink and drown. Instead you relax, and float."*
>
> *Alan Watts*

What does God want? This is a pretty significant question. I have asked it many times. And I've gotten a lot of different answers: He wants obedience, He wants purity, He wants surrender, He wants repentance, He wants your sole devotion, He wants adherence to a set of rules. But over time, as I tried to give Him these things, I became more and more frustrated – more discouraged. It seemed that what I had been taught – was being taught – more than anything, said that He demanded performance. He wanted us to follow the rules. But that seemed to push me back under the Law and the expectations were always a little fuzzy. Was my performance good enough? It never seemed like it was. I was constantly disappointed in myself. What about grace? As I began to see the Law versus Grace Paradigm, as discussed in chapter three, I moved away from the concept that He expected performance – or I tried to. But that left the question, "What exactly *does* He want?

And I kind of gave up even trying after a while. Every effort I had made to adhere to the list of things given by the church leaders as necessary never seemed to get me to a place where I felt accepted – or to the place where I felt God was even just okay with me. I was at a place where I would settle for being tolerated, even if He was not necessarily pleased. And then this verse quietly but persistently came to mind.

> *"But without faith it is impossible to please Him, for he who comes to God must believe that He is, and that He is a rewarder of those who diligently seek Him."*
>
> *Hebrews 11:6 NKJV*

So, it is impossible to please Him without faith. Then faith is what He wants. Okay. But the next question was: Faith in what, exactly? I know that may sound strange, but the teachings I have had over the years in various churches got a little confusing on this point. I was taught that if I did not receive what I was believing for, it was because my faith was not strong enough. I was taught that if I said that I had tried and it didn't work, the real issue was that *I* was tried and *I* didn't work. And I was again frustrated and discouraged because it seemed that no matter what the issue was, my faith was not strong enough. It seemed my faith would never be strong enough. And then I began to realize that maybe, the problem was not the strength of my faith. Maybe the problem was where I was aiming my faith. To explain, let's look at the various things I was taught I should have faith in.

The first one I'm going to look at was a tough one. I was taught to have faith in the Bible. I'm sure that all of us that have been in church have been taught to have faith in the Bible. I had been taught that the Bible was the infallible, inerrant Word of God. I was taught that it was Holy and that every verse could stand alone and be used to teach.

> *"In the beginning was the Word, and the Word was with God, and the Word was God. He was in the beginning with God. All things were made through Him, and without Him nothing was made that was made. In*

> *Him was life, and the life was the light of men. And the light shines in the darkness, and the darkness did not comprehend it."*
>
> *John 1:1-5 NKJV*

When this passage was read, I was taught that it meant that since Jesus was the Word, then the Bible, as the Word of God, was a representation of Jesus, Himself, and should be given the same respect as Him. And I believed it. And my focus was entirely on the Bible.

As time went on and I saw verses being used to teach things that brought people under control of the Law, I began to have doubts. I was a little scared. Doubting what I had been taught about the Bible felt like doubting the entire foundation of my faith. And in a way, I guess it was. A pastor stated that the King James Version was the best word for word translation of the Bible and should therefore be the final authority on disputes in translation. And I accepted this….then the thought came, "*Wait, what? Disputes? What disputes?*" And the underlying uneasiness about my faith grew, but I tried to ignore it. You see, I had never given a lot of thought to the fact that there were dozens of English translations alone. I had always just assumed that the differences were just in updating for modern language.

At this point, I came across some writings that talked about how the Bible came to be in the form that we have it. And I discovered that often, new translations were created because someone thought that previous translations were in error. What? But the Bible is supposed to be inerrant! So I started comparing translations and found that there were some serious disagreements concerning the translation and meaning of some verses. Some translations left words out. And some translations left entire passages – or even books – out. And all of this made me very uncomfortable – again. And I laid it aside…at least I tried. But I could not look at what I learned and still believe the Bible as I had it was infallible and inerrant. These things proved that it was fallible and errant – I had to acknowledge this if I wanted to remain honest with myself. And I moved from uncomfortable to frightened. I was afraid of the truth….and became afraid of the Bible.

And then the question rose in me: what is the Word of God? I began to think about the places in the Bible where the Word of God is referenced. I looked them up. And I began to realize that when the Bible refers to the Word of God, it is not talking about itself. No. It is talking about when God spoke. Okay.

> *"But herein is the Bible itself greatly wronged. It nowhere lays claim to be regarded as the Word, the Way, the Truth. The Bible leads us to Jesus, the inexhaustible, the ever unfolding Revelation of God. It is Christ 'in whom are hid all the treasures of wisdom and knowledge,' not the Bible, save as leading to him."*
>
> *George MacDonald*

> *"It is Christ Himself, not the Bible, who is the true word of God. The Bible, read in the right spirit and with the guidance of good teachers, will bring us to Him. We must not use the Bible as a sort of encyclopedia out of which texts can be taken for use as weapons."*
>
> *C. S. Lewis*

These statements by Christian men that I greatly respected cracked the shell of the teachings I had grown up with. I began to see that it was possible to let go of the teachings I grew up with concerning the Bible and still hold onto faith. I began to see how I had been taught to dismantle the Bible into pieces – dissect the very life out of it. I saw that this allowed passages – verses – to be taken out of context and used to preach whatever the speaker wanted to preach. And we couldn't question because the Bible was quoted and it was infallible. And now the question that arose in me was: What is the purpose of the Bible?

As I pondered this, I realized that in declaring the Bible as the Word of God, I was elevating it to being equal with God – to being as important as Jesus. But the Bible is not God. The Bible is a created thing. God inspired? Yes. Breathed to the writers by the Holy Spirit? Absolutely. Equal with God? No! I realized that the events in the Bible are not true because they are recorded in the Bible. No. The Bible is true because the events recorded in the Bible actually happened. The Bible does not make God true, God makes the Bible true. This is a big difference. I realized that I had been placing my faith in the Bible. We should not follow and worship the Bible. The purpose of the Bible is not to be worshipped – and by claiming it as the infallible, inerrant Word of God, I was elevating it to worship status. There is only One who is inerrant and infallible: God, Himself. Anything, no matter how inspired by God, which passes through human hands, is subject to fallibility because man is not infallible – only God can claim that. I began to see that the purpose of the Bible is not to be worshipped – not to be served. Its purpose is to serve. It is a God given tool to explain God's plan to us, to reveal God to us, to teach us about God, to point us to Jesus. That is its sole and very vitally important purpose. There is no greater purpose. It is a witness to God's plan and involvement in the life of His creation. But it is still just a created tool and should never be elevated to equality with God. Even if the Bible is not perfect, God is an expert at perfectly using all things. I realized that if the purpose of studying the Bible is to prove myself right and others wrong, I was acting like a spiritual two year old – or worse, a spiritual sociopath. With this understanding, I was no longer afraid of the Bible – it could no longer be used as a weapon against me.

Okay. I had settled that faith in the Bible was not what God was after. But the question still remained: What do I have faith in? It still seemed a bit complicated. The teachings I had received told me that I should ask God for what I needed – or wanted – and if I believed I would receive it, I would. So…faith in receiving. It was said that I should have faith for health, faith for prosperity, faith for whatever it was that I wanted or needed. But I ran into the same problem. Most of the time, it didn't seem to work. Not for me. And not for most people I knew. What was I missing? I was told that the problem was that I was just not believing hard enough – that I was not *really* in faith or it would manifest. I found myself back in the place of not being good enough. I tried. I stepped out 'in faith' for things and fell flat on my face. And I felt that I just couldn't get it right. It was very discouraging. Depressing. Maybe I wasn't even *really* a believer. And the church I was in placed the blame on me for any and all 'faith failures.' And then I was exposed to the abuses of power within the church. And I walked away. I decided that I just could not understand this faith thing and I could not be around people who condemned me for that while using their power and position to harm people. I thought I was done. My faith felt very weak.

But God is persistent, loving, faithful – He does not leave us in the dark. He may lead us into a dark place, but He will not leave us there. During this time, I could not even read the Bible because when I did, all I heard was the teachings of condemnation I had been taught. For several years, the only prayer I could really say with any heart in it was simply, "Papa, help." And that was enough. He did. He said, "Relax and trust Me." Gently, He led me to places where I was accepted. Slowly, I began to trust again. Through this time, God began to talk to me – through others that were earning my trust – and directly. He began telling me what He was going to do for me – what He was doing in me. He began giving me promises. And I wrote them down. And kept them tucked away. For years. And even began to forget them. I didn't have the energy to try and believe for them. Then I heard this: When God gives a promise – a prophecy – for your future, it is not your job to bring it to pass; the 'bringing it to pass' part is God's job. Oh. Wow – as that settled in me, it was a huge relief. I don't have to make His words come to pass. Good. Because I had already found that I couldn't, no matter how hard I tried. And He said, "Relax and trust Me."

Over time, as He rebuilt my faith, I began to realize something. Back to the question: What does He want? Yes, faith is what He wants. Not faith in a program, or a book, or a person, or a doctrine, or an organization, or a group. No.

> "And he believed in the LORD, and He accounted it to him for righteousness."
> *Genesis 15:6 NKJV*

Abraham did not believe the Bible, or even the Tanakh (the Jewish Scriptures). They did not exist yet. Abraham believed God. When God spoke to Abraham, Abraham believed Him. Not because some book or preacher or doctrine told him to. No, Abraham believed God because He knew God. He had a relationship with God and because of God's demonstrated character to Abraham and his ancestors, Abraham trusted God. Ah…

Have faith in God, Himself – Jesus. As this dawned on me, I realized that I had spent a good deal of my life having faith in things and ideas, instead of God, Himself. I had been taught a lot of sure-fire formulas for getting your faith to work. But here's the thing about formulas: If they are valid – if they are true – they will work every time without fail. Period. Every mathematical formula works every time, no faith required. Every chemical formula works every time, no matter the level of understanding of the person following the formula, even if the person doesn't believe in chemistry and that the formula will work, it still works. Therefore, if the formulas or recipes that are being sold as sure fire ways to get spiritual results are true, they would work every time for everyone who follows them, regardless of what they believe.

But God is not a formula to be followed. He is not a recipe to be adhered to. He is not a set of rules or steps that, if done in sequence, guarantee the desired outcome. No. God is a person. He is the Creator of all things. He is our Father. He does not want the blind, faithless following of rules – or blind faith *in* the rules. He wants relationship –

ongoing, growing, deepening relationship. And from that relationship, trust – faith – in Him develops and grows. Not faith in what He may do, or faith in our ability to follow a set of rules, or faith in a specific event or outcome. No. Faith in Him, as a person, as our Creator Father. Not even faith in His promises alone, but faith in Him who made the promises. God is not trustworthy because of His promise. His promise is trustworthy because He is God. Have hope in the promises because you have faith in God. Works are not how you please God. Faith is. Faith in what? Your works? No. The Bible? No. Faith in *Him*. Faith in His character – who He is. The works – that is, the fruit of the Spirit – follows the simple, child-like faith in Christ – in God – in Abba, Father, Papa. That is *all.* We lay aside all of our own works and look at Him. His works will follow us when we follow *Him*.

> *"Then Job answered the LORD and said:*
> *"I know that You can do everything,*
> *And that no purpose of Yours can be withheld from You.*
> *You asked, 'Who is this who hides counsel without knowledge?'*
> *Therefore I have uttered what I did not understand,*

Things too wonderful for me, which I did not know.
Listen, please, and let me speak;
You said, 'I will question you, and you shall answer Me.'
"I have heard of You by the hearing of the ear,
But now my eye sees You.
Therefore I abhor myself,
And repent in dust and ashes.""

Job 42:1-6 NKJV

"With what shall I come before the LORD,
And bow myself before the High God?
Shall I come before Him with burnt offerings,
With calves a year old?
Will the LORD be pleased with thousands of rams,
Ten thousand rivers of oil?
Shall I give my firstborn for my transgression,
The fruit of my body for the sin of my soul?
He has shown you, O man, what is good;
And what does the LORD require of you
But to do justly,
To love mercy,
And to walk humbly with your God?"

Micah 6:6-8 NKJV

"Blessed is that man who makes the LORD his trust,

And does not respect the proud, nor such as turn aside to lies.
Many, O LORD my God, are Your wonderful works
Which You have done;
And Your thoughts toward us
Cannot be recounted to You in order;
If I would declare and speak of them,
They are more than can be numbered.
Sacrifice and offering You did not desire;
My ears You have opened.
Burnt offering and sin offering You did not require."

Psalm 40:4-6 NKJV

"For I desire mercy and not sacrifice,
And the knowledge of God more than burnt offerings."

Hosea 6:6 NKJV

"But regarding anything beyond this, dear friend, go easy. There's no end to the publishing of books, and constant study wears you out so you're no good for anything else. The last and final word is this:

Fear God.
Do what he tells you.

And that's it. Eventually God will bring everything that we do out into the open and

judge it according to its hidden intent,
whether it's good or evil."
Ecclesiastes 12:12-14 The Message

First, we learn about God. But then we must know God. In the end, the endless study and reading of books is the exercise of learning about God. And there is nothing wrong with studying to learn about God. But it is not the same thing as knowing God, first hand. What does God want? He is not looking for ever increasing sacrifice that leads to a sense of self-congratulation. He is not looking for us to earn our way through endless study. Faith in what we've been taught and studied about God will not stand when crises come. Faith born of relationship will. Knowing about God won't save us. Knowing Him and being known by Him is the thing. Knowing Him enough to relax and trust Him – trust Him enough to rest in Him – trust Him enough to relax and turn all of our outcomes over to Him. That is the point. That is what He wants.

"Faith is a living, daring confidence in
God's grace, so sure and certain that a man
could stake his life on it a thousand times."
Martin Luther

God, who am I?

> *"...I've heard it described thus: much of historical church teaching in the West has presented us as sinners in need of salvation. But the Gospel goes further, and describes us as orphans in need of adoption."*
>
> *Nick Bulbeck*

Who am I? I think this is a question everyone asks, sooner or later. And it is an important question. What we believe about who we are affects how we approach everything in life. In previous chapters, we have discussed who God is and what He is like – at least to our limited ability to comprehend. We have discussed what being a Christian is at its core and what He wants. But within all of that, the question still percolates: Who am I?

> *"For now we see but a faint reflection of riddles and mysteries as though reflected in a mirror, but one day we will see face-to-face. My understanding is incomplete now, but one day I will understand everything, just as everything about me has been fully understood."*
>
> *1 Corinthians 13:12 TPT*

How to explain who we are? It is a bit daunting. Just as we are not capable of fully comprehending who God is, so we are not yet able to fully understand who we are. But to begin, I'll touch on who we are not.

Growing up, the teaching I received tended to convey the idea that we were worthless until God saved us. But when I pondered this idea, it didn't really hold up. The worth of something is determined by the price someone is willing to pay for it. Jesus was willing to give His life for us – before we even were born. I'd say we are not created without worth.

> *"Then God saw everything that He had made, and indeed it was very good. So the evening and the morning were the sixth day."*
>
> *Genesis 1:31 NKJV*

This says that God deemed what He created – including us – not just good, but *very* good. So why do so many churches, in my experience, teach the concept that we are vile, worthless worms without God? It seems that somehow, the idea has crept in that if people aren't made to feel worthless and afraid, they won't turn to God. But as I studied, it seemed to me that a confession of faith coerced out of fear might not hold once the person was outside the influence of the church that told them they were worthless.

> *"Do the riches of his extraordinary kindness make you take him for granted and despise him? Haven't you experienced how kind and understanding he has been to you? Don't mistake his tolerance for acceptance. Do you realize that all the wealth of his extravagant kindness is meant to melt your heart and lead you into repentance?"*
>
> *Romans 2:4 TPT*

I realized that contrary to what I grew up hearing, we do not come to a place of genuinely and deeply wanting to turn from what we have been doing and turn to follow Jesus out of fear and intimidation. It is His goodness – His Love – that brings us to that place of true gratitude and self-awareness. God does not look down on us as ants nor does He consider us worthless. He created us good. Am I saying we are perfect? Absolutely not. Anyone who looks at themselves honestly will acknowledge that they do things they know full well they shouldn't – often. It is part of having the freedom to choose – day by day, minute by minute – what we are going to do and who we are going to follow. And like children, we are on a learning curve. The more we know, the more is expected of us. But like children, sometimes we just say no. We rebel against the instruction of our Father. And without His instruction and help, we will never grow into what He made us to be. And this brings me back to the question: who are we?

> *"So we are convinced that every detail of our lives is continually woven together to fit into God's perfect plan of bringing good into our lives, for we are his lovers who have been called to fulfill his designed purpose. For he knew all about us before we were born and he destined us from the beginning to share the likeness of his Son. This means the Son is the oldest among a vast family of brothers and sisters who will become just like him."*
>
> *Romans 8:28-29 TPT*

I think that most of us who grew up in church or have been around church for any length of time have heard "we are all children of God," in some form. And it is true. If we are followers of Christ – if we have turned from whatever we were following and started following Him – then we *are* made children of God. But what does this mean?

A difficulty for me that I had to wrestle with was that as a child growing up in an abusive environment, I didn't know how that translated into being a child of God. It was not an easy concept for me to understand that God, as a loving Father, actually liked me – was actually on my side and wanting good for me. And so there was a major disconnect that made it very easy for me to believe that God, even though He was my Father, merely tolerated me because He was obligated to. I lived my Christian faith for many years under this basic premise – and the teachings I received in various churches seemed to only reinforce this idea – we are all sinners one step away from destruction. The focus was on us and our inability to get it right (with an undercurrent of expectation that we should). The more I studied and came to realize the Love of God and the relationship of Law and Grace, the more I began to realize that what I knew about being a child – and what seemed to be taught in church – didn't seem to fit. And I longed for that relationship that I seemed to see described – that I sensed from deep inside was available. For a long time, the fear of getting an answer that would mess with my religious beliefs prevented me from allowing myself to question. But the questions would not be quiet. And so, for intense periods – interspersed with long bouts of hiding – I studied. I read. And as I saw more and more, I realized that the church that taught me not to tolerate myself was, in fact, not to be trusted – and I questioned. And I questioned. And I realized that maybe being in a place of asking questions was actually a good and even healthy place to be. And this grew loud in me: God's core character is Love – and at the heart of Love is choice. Those who serve because they have no choice do not serve out of love. But those who choose, out of love to serve, serve with passion.

> *"Don't you realize that grace frees you to choose your own master? But choose carefully, for you surrender yourself to become a servant—bound to the one you choose to obey. If you choose to love sin, it will become your master, and it will own you and reward you with death. But if you choose to love and obey God, he will lead you into perfect righteousness."*
>
> *Romans 6:15 TPT*

In chapter one, we explored one of the first things born of that questioning – God's foundational character is Love. And the realization that this has to be the foundation if the relationship is going to be healthy. And in chapters two, three, and four, we saw that we often place our focus on the wrong things – on ourselves and our efforts instead of on Jesus and what He succeeded in doing. I come back to the question, "who am I?"

> *"And since we are his true children, we qualify to share all his treasures, for indeed, we are heirs of God himself. And since we are joined to Christ, we also inherit all that he is and all that he has. We will experience being co-glorified with him provided that we accept his suffering as our own."*
>
> *Romans 8:17 TPT*

Okay. This is a really big statement. So big that for many years, I just glossed over it when I read it because within the worm paradigm, it just did *not* compute. But the reality is, throughout the Scriptures, we are referred to as being God's children. But what does that really mean? In living my day to day life, what does it mean to be His daughter?

Well, to get an idea, let's look at a human example. In Medieval Europe, the nations were ruled by kings. The king's power was absolute. He held the power of life and death in his hand. He also held the responsibility of maintaining and protecting his kingdom. And his subjects either feared or loved him, depending on his temperament – what kind of king he was. For this example, we will say that the king is a good king – wise, merciful, just. He cares about his kingdom and the people in it. So where would we fit in this picture? As children of the king, we are invested with his authority. That is to say, people understand that when they are dealing with us, they are dealing with the king, himself. We are given a ring with the symbol of the king on it – a signet ring. Whenever someone questions our authority, showing that signet silences all questions. The signet represents the full authority of the king and any who wear it – especially those who wear the familial version of it (as opposed to advisors or ministers) – are to be treated as if they were the king, himself. As I began to really think about this, it kind of scared me. Does God really see us this way?

"Those who truly love me are those who obey my commands. Whoever passionately loves me will be passionately loved by my Father. And I will passionately love you in return and will manifest my life within you."
John 14:21 TPT

"So then, we must cling in faith to all we know to be true. For we have a magnificent King-Priest, Jesus Christ, the Son of God, who rose into the heavenly realm for us, and now sympathizes with us in our frailty. He understands humanity, for as a Man, our magnificent King-Priest was tempted in every way just as we are, and conquered sin. So now we come freely and boldly to where love is enthroned, to receive mercy's kiss and discover the grace we urgently need to strengthen us in our time of weakness."
Hebrews 4:14-16 TPT

"But those who embraced him and took hold of his name were given authority to become the children of God!"
John 1:12 TPT

"The Holy Spirit of God has sealed you in Jesus Christ until you experience your full salvation. So never grieve the Spirit of God or take for granted his holy influence in your life."
Ephesians 4:30 TPT

And the more I studied, the stronger this image became. I am a daughter of God, loved and trusted – with access to my Father's very throne. As His daughter, within His kingdom, I have His authority backing me. Wow. We have been made children of the King within the Kingdom of God. Within the realm of the spirit, which is a higher realm that the realm of the physical, we are children of the King of all spirits and have the authority of that place.

> *"But God still loved us with such great love. He is so rich in compassion and mercy. Even when we were dead and doomed in our many sins, he united us into the very life of Christ and saved us by his wonderful grace! He raised us up with Christ the exalted One, and we ascended with him into the glorious perfection and authority of the heavenly realm, for we are now co-seated as one with Christ!"*
>
> *Ephesians 2:4-6 TPT*

> *"For it was always in his perfect plan to adopt us as his delightful children, through our union with Jesus, the Anointed One, so that his tremendous love that cascades over us would glorify his grace—for the same love he has for his Beloved One, Jesus, he*

has for us. And this unfolding plan brings him great pleasure!"

Ephesians 1:5-6 TPT

This was exciting! Is this how He really sees me? Sees you? And His response was: Yes!

"But when that era came to an end and the time of fulfillment had come, God sent his Son, born of a woman, born under the written law. Yet all of this was so that he would redeem and set free all those held hostage to the written law so that we would receive our freedom and a full legal adoption as his children. And so that we would know for sure that we are his true children, God released the Spirit of Sonship into our hearts—moving us to cry out intimately, "My Father! You're our true Father!" Now we're no longer living like slaves under the law, but we enjoy being God's very own sons and daughters! And because we're his, we can access everything our Father has—for we are heirs of God through Jesus, the Messiah!"

Galatians 4:4-7 TPT

It says "full legal adoption." And then I discovered that adoption in the Near East 2,000 years ago was not the same as it is today. Today, when we think of adoption, we think of an orphan or someone who has been removed from abusive parents being adopted to give them a new family – a new home. And that is well and fine and paints a nice picture…but it is by no means the whole of what it meant then. Then, to adopt someone usually had nothing to do with whether or not they had parents of their own. And it mostly was adults who were adopted. To adopt someone meant that you were taking them into your family and giving them the legal right to inheritance equal with your first born – and in their culture, the first born got the larger inheritance. And in their culture, the natural born sons could be disinherited…but an adopted son was permanent. Once the adoption was legally done, it could not be revoked. Think about the fact that we are heirs…with Christ! This is almost overwhelming…

But then another question arose: How does this being a child of God square with all the passages that talk about being God's servant? I grew up hearing much more about being a servant of God than a child. The arguments I heard went something like this: you are a servant of God or you are nothing – being a child of God is just the icing on the cake. Okay. Well, no – not okay. Is that how you treat your children? I hope not. And as I continued to dig and wrestle with this – am I His child or His servant? – the analogy of the medieval kingdom came back to mind. It is something that can still be observed in European royal families even now. When the king is a good, wise, just king, his children love him. And although they have been invested with his authority so that when they are out in the kingdom, they are respected as the king himself, because they love their father and his kingdom, they want to help. They serve the kingdom out of love for their father. Although they are not servants, out of love for their father and his kingdom, they take on the mantle of a servant – willingly and gladly. Why? Because of that love – they want to see their father's kingdom prosper. The medieval concept of *noblesse oblige* came to mind. It is an old French term that literally translates *nobility obligates.* The concept was, simply put, that those who were of noble, or royal, birth had an obligation to watch out for and care for those within their kingdom who were poor or orphaned or unable to care for themselves – to act with honor. This is, I think, a pale reflection of the way God's kingdom works.

Just as it is with the above described children, so it is with us – with me. I love my Father. The more I know Him and understand who He is and what He has done for me, the more I love Him and want to do whatever He asks. I want to see His kingdom grow and prosper. I want to see more people come to know Him the way I do and experience His love the way I do. And I realized that this is what Peter was talking about – at least in part – in his first letter.

> *"But you are a chosen generation, a royal priesthood, a holy nation, His own special people, that you may proclaim the praises of Him who called you out of darkness into His marvelous light; who once were not a people but are now the people of God, who had not obtained mercy but now have obtained mercy."*
>
> *1 Peter 2:9-10 NKJV*

In this, we are both kings and priests – kings (or heirs) *and* priests (or servants). And in realizing this, I realized that being a daughter of the highest King, of God, and being His servant were not contradictory. He makes me a child out of

His love, and out of my love for Him I choose to serve. But I still remain His child, with all the authority that He has given me through that. I am His priest gladly, but I am His daughter, first.

> *"And you did not receive the "spirit of religious duty," leading you back into the fear of never being good enough. But you have received the "Spirit of full acceptance," enfolding you into the family of God. And you will never feel orphaned, for as he rises up within us, our spirits join him in saying the words of tender affection, "Beloved Father!" For the Holy Spirit makes God's fatherhood real to us as he whispers into our innermost being, "You are God's beloved child!"*
>
> *Romans 8:15-16 TPT*

And yes, it is sometimes hard to serve. There are times that He has asked me to do things that flat out hurt. But I have found that the more time I spend with Him – the more I get to know Him – the more I love and trust Him. And the more I love Him and the more I trust him, the more it becomes easier to do what He asks and harder to tell Him no.

So, who am I? I am a daughter of the King of all kings. Who are you? If you are a follower of Jesus, you are a son or daughter of the King of all kings…and my brother – my sister.

> *"Then Jesus called a little child to Him, set him in the midst of them, and said, "Assuredly, I say to you, unless you are converted and become as little children, you will by no means enter the kingdom of heaven."*
>
> *Matthew 18:2-3 NKJV*

Made in the USA
Monee, IL
04 February 2021

59648719R00049